JO DRAI

POST-MEDIEVAL
POTTERY
1650-1800

SHIRE ARCHAEOLOGY

2

Published in 2001 by
SHIRE PUBLICATIONS LTD
Cromwell House, Church Street, Princes Risborough,
Buckinghamshire HP27 9AA, UK.
Website: www.shirebooks.co.uk

Series Editor: James Dyer

Number 40 in the Shire Archaeology series.

ISBN 0 85263 681 4

First published 1984; reprinted 2001.

Printed in Great Britain by
CIT Printing Services Ltd, Press Buildings,
Merlins Bridge, Haverfordwest, Pembrokeshire SA61 1XF.

Contents

4

Acknowledgements

I am very grateful to Robert Charleston, who kindly read the typescript and removed many blemishes; and to Christopher Chaplin for all his help and for his drawings of the pottery group. Numbers 15-17 were drawn by Daphne Roscoe, and I thank her for permission to reproduce them. I thank Northampton Museum, Dorset County Museum, the Fitzwilliam Museum, Cambridge, the Royal Albert Memorial Museum, Exeter, and Temple Newsam House, Leeds, for the photographs. I am grateful to the late Louis Lipski, to Peter Walton and to Robert Charleston for identifying many of the Northampton pots and to W. N. Terry, curator of Northampton Museum; Keith Clulow of Fotographic Northampton for all the Northampton photographs; Pam McClintock for splendid typing; and Mrs B. M. Draper, Roger Peers and Jeany Poulsen for advice on the typescript and removing some of the grammatical blunders. The blemishes which remain are my own.

The publishers acknowledge the advice of Robert Copeland in the preparation of this book.

By the end of the eighteenth century there was a great contrast between porcelain and earthenwares — the slipware plate is the later. **1.** Worcester porcelain painted in a classical style, and many colours, possibly in London, around the 1770s (diameter 214 mm). **2.** Slipware plate dated 1796, made at an unknown country pottery (diameter 216 mm). Both about a quarter actual size. (Northampton Museum.)

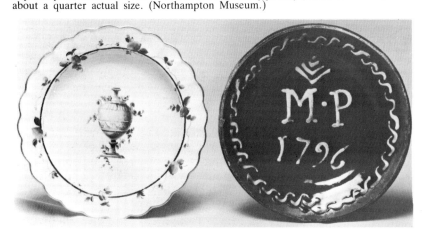

1
Introduction

The years 1650 to 1800 cover the most interesting period of English pottery production: new methods, fabrics and shapes were being developed or imported all the time, and an enormous variety of pots of a very high standard was produced.

The pottery of this period has been approached from two standpoints. The art-historical approach is based on current collections of pottery, consisting of pots which have survived because, they were special, being either of high quality like porcelain or fine earthenwares, or with inscriptions, as with much of the surviving earthenware. However, archaeologically excavated material shows a very different emphasis, with the bulk of the material up to the early or mid nineteenth century being locally produced plain or very simply decorated earthenwares. These common pots were used, broken and discarded in great quantities, rarely surviving whole to be collected. The small quantities of finer wares found in the archaeological groups are, however, most valuable, as these were far more responsive to fashion and to technological change. They are therefore easier to date closely than the conservative earthenwares. I have tried to use both sources here, but inevitably the finer wares have predominated simply because they change so much. As an archaeological survey this is incomplete: earthenwares vary from county to county, so that the small sample here represents only a tiny fraction of the variety produced.

Many of the types of pottery illustrated here were in production at the same time and were either aimed at different levels of the market or performed different functions. For example, porcelain was used for fine tea and coffee services (1), while plain locally made earthenwares (2) were being used in the kitchen and dairy, and stonewares in the cellar. Many other materials could be used for the same purposes as pottery: silver and glass competed with porcelain at the upper end of the market, while brass, pewter, wood, leather and iron competed with earthenwares at the lower end. These materials all influenced pottery styles, as did imports of all types. Contemporary pottery imports are mentioned in the text but generally not illustrated, owing to lack of space. Figures and other purely decorative forms receive little mention.

Until the invention in Staffordshire, in the mid eighteenth

century, of creamware, which was exported and prized all over
Europe and beyond, as the best reasonably priced pottery of the
period, Britain had been a backwater for ceramic production.
British ceramics were influenced by continental developments
and seldom achieved the quality of, for example, tin-glazed
earthenware produced in Europe.

Local earthenware handled bowls, both excavated in Dorchester in 1898. **3.** Plain greeny
orange glaze (height 68 mm). **4.** With white slip decoration (diameter 132 mm). Probably
early eighteenth century. Both about one-third actual size. (Dorset County Museum.)

Chamber-pots, a form rarely represented in collections. **5.** With slip decoration, from the
group illustrated in chapter 9; early eighteenth century (height 148 mm). **6.** Olive green
glaze inside and splashes outside; probably later eighteenth century; local earthenware
(height 155 mm). Both about a quarter actual size. (Dorset County Museum.)

2
Local earthenwares

Archaeologically local earthenwares are often called coarse-wares, but by comparison with earlier pots they are not coarse. By comparison with delft and the later fine earthenwares they do seem so, however. Long before 1650 almost all potters were using a fine, fairly hard fabric with a little fine sand temper, which is very sophisticated by comparison with much medieval and earlier pottery tempered with large grit or ground shell. Almost all pots were at least partially glazed, whereas in the medieval period only jugs and finer vessels were glazed. Metal cooking vessels were very common and had completely replaced the simple ceramic cooking pot, which had been the commonest pottery form made from the neolithic period onwards. There was no reduction in the amount of pottery in circulation, because during the late sixteenth century, when the cooking pot was superseded, many new pottery forms such as dishes, plates, bowls (some handled), cups, mugs and specialised cooking vessels like skillets and chafing dishes came into common use. The other very common medieval form — the jug, or pitcher — continued in production, as did large storage vessels.

Almost all post-medieval earthenwares are oxidised and therefore red, because they were fired in a kiln with plenty of air, or rather oxygen, available. Many medieval wares were black or dark brown because they were fired in a reducing atmosphere, in a sealed kiln where the supply of free oxygen was limited.

All forms were made in metal, but the pottery equivalent was much cheaper. Even more economical were wooden bowls, drinking vessels and trenchers. Neither metal nor wooden vessels are well represented in archaeological deposits because wood rots away and the metal vessels were recycled by being melted down when broken beyond repair.

Probate inventories (lists of possessions made after death) show the low value placed on earthenwares since they rarely mention them at all. They do, however, clearly indicate the great variety of the more valuable metal cooking and serving vessels. An inventory of a 'gentleman' in Yetminster, Dorset, in 1686 lists '1 furnace pan, 2 brass pots, 2 kettles, 2 skillets, 2 skimmers, 2 brass ladles, a pestle and morter, 2 brass candlesticks and 2 chaffindishes' (chafing dishes) and '18 pewter dishes, 12 pewter plates, 12 pewter porringers, 3 pewter candlesticks and other small pewter salts and drinking boles, 4 pewter chamber pots, a bed pan and closestool pan', whilst any pottery he possessed must be included with 'other lumber goods'. This rich inventory gives a good idea of the variety of brass and pewter used, but any wooden vessels present would have been too cheap to be listed. A later inventory of a yeoman from Leigh, Dorset, does however list '5 trenchers and one cage', presumably because of the 'cage' or stand. This inventory of 1769 includes bell-metal, pewter and iron vessels, and '3 stone plates and some cups . . . 1 tea pot and tea dishes', which are probably included because they are not common local earthenware. Earthenwares were used, broken and discarded, so that they rarely survived to be collected, and collectors tended to concentrate on decorated wares.

Local earthenwares therefore are mostly known through the archaeological record, and here they appear in huge quantities. Even pit groups of the mid nineteenth century include a few local bowls or other kitchen wares, whilst in groups of the seventeenth and eighteenth centuries they predominate (chapter 9).

Many of the local potteries were small family concerns, and often pottery making was only a part-time occupation. Surviving accounts, wills and inventories show that the potters were often small farmers as well. Local clay was used, dug from as close to the kiln and workshop as possible. Some of these clays needed weathering in the frost or mixing with fine sand, whilst others were suitable for firing without any addition. All, however, had to have any stones or gravel removed, sometimes by diluting the clay with water until it was a slip and then sieving it. After the clay

7. Plain everyday earthenware bowl, with a brown-flecked orangey glaze inside; probably eighteenth century (height 153 mm). **8.** A very splendid twelve-handled bowl glazed greenish yellow overall; earthenware, probably made at Verwood (Dorset), and perhaps eighteenth century (height 134 mm). Both about one-sixth actual size. (Dorset County Museum.)

Local earthenwares 9

Earthenware pots with an iron-rich slip under the glaze. **9.** A very crude jug (height 182 mm). **10.** A storage vessel (height 246 mm). The slip can be seen extending below the glaze. Probably eighteenth century. Both about a quarter actual size. (Northampton Museum.)

Mugs. **11.** With a dull green glaze, from the group illustrated in chapter 9 (height 172 mm). **12.** Pale buff fabric with a streaky brown glaze (height 131 mm). Both earthenware, early eighteenth century, with bands of ridging reminiscent of metal or wooden vessels. Both about two-fifths actual size. (12: Northampton Museum.)

had been trampled or mixed and then kneaded to remove air pockets it was ready for use.

Almost all local earthenwares were thrown on the wheel, that is, formed by placing a suitably sized lump of clay on a small circular platform (wheel) and shaping the pot as this revolves. Early wheels were powered by the potter's feet, but during the eighteenth century wheels came into use that were directly cranked by another worker or driven like a lathe by cord and pulley from a large hand-turned wheel.

When the main part of the pot was leather hard the handles were attached. Pottery needs to be dry before it is fired because any water left in the body will make it shatter in the kiln. In the simplest potteries vessels were dried outside in the sun, but many had drying sheds, some using a low artificial heat.

Glazing made the pots less porous and more attractive. Originally galena, a lead ore mined at several places in England, was ground to a powder and dusted on, but a later and better method was to dip the pot in a liquid mixture of slip and galena as this could cover more of the pot. In the later seventeenth century litharge or lead oxide, which gave a shinier finish, started to replace galena, although not all local potteries changed to it. Most local potters ground and prepared their own glazes.

Some potters used saggars in the kiln, but others simply placed sherds of pottery or pellets of clay between the vessels to prevent the glaze from sticking them together. Later developments included fixed shelves inside the kiln so that the finer wares could be stacked separately. Firing makes the pot hard and turns the glaze into a shiny glass-like coating. Many different types of kiln were used at this period, varying in complexity from the simple clamp with no permanent superstructure (an early and surprisingly effective method of firing) to quite large complex kilns with a permanent dome, several firemouths, and a covered walkway around to protect the firing area from the weather. A great variety of fuels was used, ranging from wood, or even furze, to coal or peat. Firing would take from three days to a week. The temperature was raised slowly at first, to make sure the pots were wholly dry, then steadily to a maximum of around 1000 ° C. The kiln might take two or three days to cool down.

Most early pottery was produced by these processes, but for more refined wares more sophisticated methods were used, particularly for decorated pots. These are described under the appropriate type of pottery.

13. An unglazed earthenware fire pot, which would be filled with hot ashes for use as a portable heater: probably eighteenth century (height 131 mm). About one-fifth actual size. **14.** A simple slipware dish with yellowy slip and green glaze, of a type produced by many local potteries during the eighteenth and nineteenth centuries (diameter 281 mm). About one-sixth actual size. (Both Northampton Museum.)

Glaze colour results from the colour of the body of the pot or the slip coatings, seen through the basically colourless glaze, or from additions to the glaze itself. Most clays contain iron, which in an oxidising atmosphere makes the glaze orangey or brown depending on how much is present, and on some earthenwares

15. Puzzle jug with a dark brown glaze (height 172 mm). The tube in the handle supplies the nozzles on the rim. Probably nineteenth century. **16.** Posset pot with a dark brown glaze, probably made in Wiltshire, late seventeenth or early eighteenth century (height 178 mm). Both earthenware, about a quarter actual size. (15: Northampton Museum; 16: Dorset County Museum.)

iron-rich flecks in the fabric produce small brown stains in the glaze. Some of the very dark brown wares have an iron-rich slip under the glaze (this is particularly clear on 9 and 10, where the slip extends further down the pot than the glaze). Many post-medieval pots have an olive-green glaze, or one which has patches of orange and green, and this is probably the result of full or partial reduction in the kiln at the end of the firing: green or orange, or patchy, glazes were produced by the same pottery.

Instead of being applied as a slip, iron could be added directly to the glaze, and manganese was also used in this way, producing a dark brown speckled and streaked effect (12 and 21). A very good green was produced by using copper filings in the glaze, but during this period they were mostly used for very sparse flecks of green on slipwares, especially *sgraffito*.

Besides forms which are still made and used today, these potters were producing some vessels (particularly for liquids) which are less familiar. Puzzle jugs (15) of various shapes, but all using the principle of a concealed tube bypassing the pierced neck, were commonly made in both local and fine earthenwares. Fuddling cups, formed of several conjoined cups (17) made in slipware, earthenware or delft, were also designed to drench the drinker. Posset pots, for the popular drinks made from spiced hot milk with wine, beer or honey, were commonly made in delft, slipware and local earthenwares during the seventeenth and earlier eighteenth centuries (16, 25, 26 and 37).

Many of these local potteries were also producing slip-decorated wares in the same basic fabric as the plain earthenware (2, 14 and 29). Distinguishing a simple slip-decorated vessel from one which has no slip but which might well have been fired in the

17. Brown glazed earthenware fuddling cup with intertwined handles, probably made in Wiltshire; purchased in West Dorset in 1887 (height 82 mm). **18.** Earthenware skillet in fine buff fabric with a very smooth glaze varying from dark yellow to pale olive green (height 41 mm). Both probably seventeenth century, about one quarter actual size. (Dorset County Musem.)

19. Splendidly proportioned earthenware jug with an iron-rich slip producing a very dark brown glaze; late seventeenth or early eighteenth century (height 178 mm). **20.** Slipware jug washed with a white slip and with brown slip decoration, probably Staffordshire, late seventeenth century (height 174 mm). Both about one-third actual size. (Northampton Museum.)

same kiln, as this book does, might be considered silly, but sorting pots into their different types does aid our understanding of them. Fine earthenware factories also produced several types side by side.

In some cases the local earthenware potters and the fineware potters both made the same forms, such as plain bowls (7) and chamber pots (5 and 6), but generally the fineware potters of the eighteenth century concentrated on the more sophisticated forms, like tea and coffee wares, whilst the local potters supplied heavy utilitarian cheap pots. Throughout this period the local potters retained much of the market in baking, brewing and cheesemaking utensils, which were very heavy to transport. Archaeological groups indicate that they also supplied almost all of the kitchen wares. Slip-decorated pots are not necessarily better than the plain earthenwares, as demonstrated by the jugs above. Local earthenwares are occasionally dull, heavy or even ill suited to their function, but many are handsome objects, made by master craftsmen who produced huge quantities of simple cheap vessels for everyday use, highly functional, very beautiful and tʰ epitome of good design. These qualities result from the ℊ experience and skill of the individual potters, from thʳ tradition of pottery making, and perhaps from the direcᵗ between many of these potters and their customerˢ

The enormous Staffordshire industry grew out of local earthenware potteries at Burslem, initially because the area was very well supplied with a great variety of good potting clays and had a local supply of coal to fire the kilns. Improved marketing seems to have been another factor in the expansion of the Staffordshire potteries. Small merchants distributed Staffordshire wares all over Britain from the middle of the seventeenth century, whereas most of the country potters took their own wares to their local markets. The use of white clays and the expansion of the Staffordshire industry meant that during the eighteenth century more and more raw materials had to be imported, but by then the inventiveness and skill of the Staffordshire potters in producing the finer wares, as well as the presence of good coal, ensured that the industry stayed in Staffordshire. The complexity of eighteenth-century fineware production, needing decorators, mould makers, block cutters and such like, as well as potters, encouraged the industry to remain in an area where all these skills were available.

Cups excavated in Northampton. **21.** Streaky brown manganese glaze (height 60 mm). **22.** White slip with brown slip decoration (height 54 mm). Both were probably made in Staffordshire although 21 could be a local product; late seventeenth century. Both about two-fifths actual size. (Northampton Museum.)

3
Slipware

Trailed slipware

Slip is clay diluted with water to form a thick liquid, which is used in various ways for decorating earthenware pots. It can be simply trailed directly on to the vessel (23 and 24) or trailed on to a complete wash of a contrasting slip (25 and 26). A plain wash was also used. The washes completely conceal the earthenware body of the pot.

The earlier types of slipware had slip patterns laid directly on the body of the pot, as with the Wrotham tyg (23). The more sophisticated wares such as 25 and 26 have dark and light slips forming the decoration and completely masking the fabric. Sometimes three slip colours were used (27), usually the natural clay colours of white, tan and dark brown, although occasionally white clay stained green was used. For the common 'combed' slip parallel lines were trailed on to a pot already coated with a different colour and a hard brush or comb was drawn across all or part of them (26). Wider trails of slip, sometimes in several colours, were used to produce beautiful marbled effects. All the slip colours are slightly altered by glazing, for example white changing to yellowy white because of the lead in the glaze.

Decoration in contrasting clays was used on medieval pottery, either as pellets or strips, or painted on, but the effects produced are different from those on post-medieval slipware. Cistercian ware, made in north-east England and the Midlands from the sixteenth century, includes dark vessels decorated with white slip, and *vice versa*. This seems to have developed into a primitive kind of slipware which itself led into the fully developed slipwares of Staffordshire. At ports, imported slipware, like the very bright dishes decorated with cockerels which came from Holland, are found from the later sixteenth century, and they may have had some influence on the development of English slipware.

Two types of early slipware have been collected because they are elaborately decorated, although only with white slip trailed directly on to the body. From Wrotham in Kent came dark browr wares decorated with pads of clay as well as with trails. Thᵣ were made alongside more utilitarian wares from the ᵣ seventeenth century (23). Besides tygs like the one illuᵣ elaborate candlesticks, globular cups and, less commᵣ

23. Wrotham slipware tyg (handled drinking vessel), with pads of white clay and trailed white slip, plaited red and white clay on the handles, and dark brown glaze; it has initials and is dated 1663 (height 187 mm). **24.** Metropolitan slipware jug with the inscription *FOR EARTH I AM;* mid seventeenth century (height 127 mm). Both about one-third actual size. (Fitzwilliam Museum, Cambridge.)

and plates were made in this elaborate style. Many are dated and bear initials which must be those of the potters as the same ones recur.

Many simpler orange-bodied slipware pots have been found in London and so are called 'Metropolitan' slipware. This was made at Harlow and elsewhere from the early seventeenth century. Dishes, jugs (24), tygs and chamber pots were decorated with

Staffordshire slipware posset pots. **25.** With a coating of dark brown slip and white decoration, and inscribed *RICHARD MIER 1699* (height 124 mm). **26.** With a coating of white slip and dark brown decoration, and inscribed *GOD BLESS QVEN ANN,* who reigned from 1702 to 1714 (height 144 mm). Both are about one quarter actual size. (Northampton Museum.)

27. Very large slipware dish with a coating of white slip and trailed decoration in dark brown slip 'jewelled' with white and with tan slip infilling; Staffordshire, about 1670-80 (diameter 450 mm). About one-sixth actual size. (Fitzwilliam Museum, Cambridge.)

simple trailed patterns and some have inscriptions. Many are religious — *FEARE GOD 1630, FAST AND PRAY 1659* — although some are secular — *BE MERE AND WIS.*

Slipware was one of the first stages through which North Staffordshire became the largest pottery-producing area in the world. During the early to mid seventeenth century earthenwares made there were distributed over an increasingly large area, and from around 1660 quantities of sophisticated slipware were produced.

Many of the Staffordshire slipwares (and the very similar wares made in Bristol) have a complete coating of slip, with the decoration in a second colour. The most magnificent have three colours, like the huge George Taylor dish (27), which is also 'jewelled', that is, many of the lines of slip have dots of white slip on them. This jewelling is also found on simpler vessels (26).

The very large dishes like 27 are the peak of the slipware potters' art. They are very difficult to throw on the wheel because they are so large, and the trailed decoration shows complete mastery of this awkward technique. Thomas Toft is the most famous name associated with these dishes, but there are several other names which recur. It is unclear whether the names are owners' or the potters', but the latter seems probable. They from about 1680 until just into the eighteenth centu

The Toft type dishes are the most elaborate slipwares ever made, but they were only a tiny proportion of production. Even in Staffordshire the bulk of slipware produced was fairly simple. Many dated or inscribed pots were made, however, including simple mugs, model cradles (presumably christening gifts), posset pots like 25 and 26 (at least some of which originally had domed lids) and dishes. Simpler slipware without the overall wash was also made in Staffordshire but was not distributed over such a wide area. Staffordshire coated slipware is found all over Britain and occurs in almost every archaeological group of appropriate date, but there were many other kilns producing slipware. Indeed, by the middle of the seventeenth century, simple locally produced slipwares are found in most excavated groups. They are mostly utilitarian wares with only sparse decoration. As everyday pots they are used, broken and discarded in large quantities, and they did not survive to be collected.

Ticknall in Derbyshire is known from documentary sources to have produced much slipware, but this can only be distinguished from Staffordshire products if, like 30, the pot is known to have been purchased near Ticknall. This is not a satisfactory method of identification. Slipware cups and dishes remarkably similar to Staffordshire wares were produced in Bristol from about 1680 and are commonly found in the south-west of England.

During the eighteenth century many local kilns produced slipware, some decorated with slip lines or simply coated with slip, some with more complex decoration, and others, particularly simple dishes, with swirled or combed decoration. These were produced in great quantities alongside plain earthenwares, throughout the eighteenth century and well into the nineteenth,

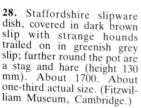

28. Staffordshire slipware dish, covered in dark brown slip with strange hounds trailed on in greenish grey slip; further round the pot are a stag and hare (height 130 mm). About 1700. About one-third actual size. (Fitzwilliam Museum, Cambridge.)

Moulded slipware dishes, both with trailed white slip. **29.** Huge simple rectangular dish, eighteenth or nineteenth century, white slip over dark brown slip (433 mm across longest side). **30.** Charming circular dish, early eighteenth century, bought near Ticknall about 1894; white slip directly on the body (diameter 322 mm). Both about one-sixth actual size. (Northampton Museum.)

31. Slipware dish made in an elaborate mould, coated with white slip and partially decorated with dark brown and tan slips which are restrained by the moulded lines (diameter 435 mm). SM on the panel in the centre is probably the mould maker's initials. Staffordshire, early to mid eighteenth century. About one-sixth actual size. (Fitzwilliam Museum, Cambridge.)

long after Staffordshire had turned to making far more sophisticated pots and fabrics. The pots produced by the local kilns were mostly for the kitchen or dairy, not for the table, although some of the dishes and bowls may have been used for serving.

Many simple slipware dishes were made by pressing thick sheets of clay over moulds. This is called press-moulding and was used for many locally produced slipwares well into the nineteenth century. Most dishes produced this way were smooth inside and decorated with marbled or combed slip, but in Staffordshire moulds were used to produce a raised or embossed pattern on the inside of the dishes, which confined the several coloured slips within the specific areas they were applied (31), producing a very neat effect. A few of the fired clay moulds survive.

Sgraffito slipware

A different type of slipware is produced by completely covering a vessel with slip and then scratching the decoration through it, so that when glazed the surviving areas of slip and the revealed body of the pot contrast with one another. It is easier to control the result by this method than by trailing the slip, but often the naive drawing of the patterns produces strange results (33). Scratched or incised decoration without a slip coating was common in the medieval period, and sgraffito slipware was imported from

32. Staffordshire, Devon or Somerset sgraffito dish, coated in white slip and dated 1753 (diameter 368 mm). There are smudges of greeny blue in the glaze. About one-fifth actual size. (Northampton Museum.)

33. North Devon sgraffito harvest jug with the royal coat of arms and the inscription on the other side: *HARVIS IS COM ALL BISSEY / NOW IN MACKIN OF YOUR / BARLY MOW WHEN MEN DO / LABER HARD AND SWET GOOD / ALE IS FAR BETTER THAN MET / BIDEFORD APRIL 28th 1774 M+W* (height 377 mm). About a half actual size. (Royal Albert Memorial Museum, Exeter.)

34. Two sides of a North Devon sgraffito honey pot with decoration including a splendid lion and the inscription *Steal not this / pot for fear of shame / for hear you see / the owners / Name Charls Gould June the 10 1807* (height 144 mm). About one-third actual size. (Royal Albert Memorial Museum.)

France, Germany and Italy from the late sixteenth century. English potters copied these imported wares from the early seventeenth century. Many of the early wares and the cheaper everyday vessels (for example, those in the excavated group, chapter 10) were decorated while the slip coating was still wet, and the decoration was executed by incising lines rather than by removing large areas of slip, a technique which became more common from the beginning of the eighteenth century.

Although during the eighteenth century Staffordshire did produce sgraffito, including very sophisticated wares, sometimes even with an agate (multicoloured) body (page 41), the main centres of production during the seventeenth and eighteenth centuries were in the West Country, especially North Devon, Somerset and Wales. Barnstaple and Bideford were well positioned for trade with America and the West Indies, and the potteries there exported great quantities of sgraffito wares during the second half of the seventeenth century. The trade declined during the eighteenth century, probably because of the competition from finer earthenwares. Most of the export trade was in table wares (cups, dishes, jugs, bowls and so on) and the same forms are found in England. Trailed slipware was also made at Barnstaple. Many elaborate harvest jugs like 33 were made from the late seventeenth century until the nineteenth. With the decline in sgraffito production the North Devon potters concentrated on plain earthenwares. Donyatt in Somerset was from the mid seventeenth century an important centre for slipware production, including both sgraffito and trailed slip decoration. Often the sgraffito wares were further ornamented by flecks of green in the glaze, produced by copper filings. Production at Donyatt declined from the middle of the eighteenth century.

In Wales, Ewenny in the south and Buckley in the north also produced sgraffito, as did many small local potteries all over Britain, about which we have no information, apart from excavated vessels, like those in the group illustrated (chapter 9). These excavated pots are much more carelessly decorated than the more elaborate vessels which tend to survive in collections, but the dishes have very effective patterns which must have been quick to produce.

A most unusual variant of slipware was produced in Sussex in the very late eighteenth and early nineteenth centuries. Decora-

35. Both sides of a Sussex earthenware spirit flask with impressed decoration inlaid with white, including along the edge *SOUTH CHAILEY POTTREY*, dated 1800 (height 123 mm). About half actual size. (Fitzwilliam Museum, Cambridge.)

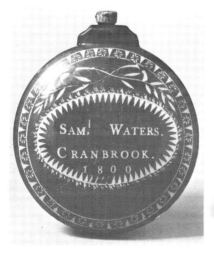

tion was impressed into the pot and then filled with slip. Printers' type was used to impress the inscriptions (35), and a neat and effective finish was achieved. Only a limited range of slip-decorated vessels was produced — most commonly spirit flasks (35), small beer barrels and tobacco jars. A characteristic inscription is *Otions of Brandy and Rivers of Wine Plantecion of Tea and a Garle to my mind.* These potteries were also producing a normal range of plain earthenwares.

Delft showing Chinese influence. **36.** Plate painted in two shades of blue with some bright yellow, in a common pattern found on several different-shaped plates; English, 1680s (diameter 192 mm). **37.** Posset pot with a slightly bluey glaze painted with dark outlining and two shades of blue; English, 1700s (height 203 mm). Both about a quarter actual size. (Northampton Museum.)

4
Delft

It would be more correct to call delft tin-glazed earthenware, but the term 'delft' is succinct and convenient and also the traditional name taken from the Dutch town, even though tin-glaze making started there long after it did in England. For delft, the usual lead glaze is made white and opaque by the addition of tin oxide, which gives a good surface on which to paint. It disguises the thick earthenware body of the pot and makes it look like porcelain.

Delft was the first white ware and the first painted coloured pottery to be produced in England. It was more complicated to produce than the common earthenwares. The pots were fired once, unglazed (biscuit firing), and then dipped in the liquid glaze. The absorbent clay took up the water, and after the biscuit dried the decoration was painted on to the surface. The difficulty of erasing a brush stroke once it had been put on added to the problems and accounts for the crudeness of some of the decoration. The pots were fired for a second time at a higher temperature to fix the colours and fuse the glaze. For this second firing the glazed vessels were placed in a large cylindrical vessel called a saggar to protect them from direct contact with the heat. Plates and dishes were kept separate from each other by triangular spurs placed between them, or later they were supported by pegs projecting inside the saggar. This prevented the glaze from fusing the vessels together. Small marks in the glaze, particularly on plates, show where these supports were used (47 and 49).

The tin needed for the glaze was supplied from Cornwall, not only to the English delft potters but to those in Holland and Italy as well. A punch bowl, probably made in Bristol and dated 1731, has the inscription *John Udy of Luxillion / his tin was so fine / it glidered this punch bowl / and made it to shine* . . . Luxulyan is in south Cornwall.

Glaze including tin oxide was used in the Middle East from at least as early as the ninth century AD, and it was first used in Europe in the twelfth century in Italy for very simple painted wares. From the thirteenth century it was used in Spain for exotic lustre painted wares. The Italian tin-glaze wares (majolica) gradually gained in sophistication until the early sixteenth century when vases and especially dishes were produced with painted decoration, often biblical or classical scenes or portraits, all of great quality.

Tin-glaze was produced in France probably from the fifteenth century; and from the late fifteenth century Holland started production, followed by other European countries during the sixteenth century.

The Dutch industry flourished and, like Italy and Spain, exported tin-glaze to England. Two potters from Antwerp are known to have set up a delft factory in Norwich and then in London, in the late sixteenth century. There are a few delft jugs, known as Malling jugs, which pre-date this and were probably made in England. They are either plain or have swirled or speckled colours, and some have silver mounts which firmly date them in the second half of the sixteenth century.

London was the main area of production of delft during the seventeenth century, with factories at Southwark from early in the century and later at Lambeth and Vauxhall. By about 1650 delft was being produced near Bristol at Brislington, and soon after in Bristol itself. The only other West Country factory was at Wincanton from about 1730 to 1750. Delft factories were set up in Liverpool in the early eighteenth century, at Glasgow in 1748, at Dublin from about 1735 and elsewhere in Ireland during the eighteenth century. Apart from Wincanton these factories went on producing delft until the 1770s, when delft was superseded by creamware.

Delft showing continental influence. **38.** Plate, dark blue overall with spattered white spots in imitation of Nevers, a French factory; late seventeenth century (diameter 218 mm). **39.** Plate painted in two shades of blue, very like Dutch tin-glaze; dated 1694 (diameter 221 mm). The animals show the influence of Italian grotesques. Both about a quarter actual size. (Northampton Museum.)

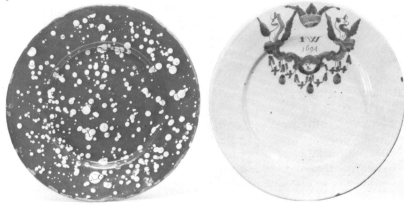

Delft drug-pots. **40** *(back).* Mid eighteenth century, with blue stripes (height 62 mm). **41, 42** *(centre).* Two with small bases, later eighteenth century, 42 with the inscription painted in manganese: *BAYLEY/COCKSPUR STREET.* **43** *(back right).* Early eighteenth century. **44** *(front left).* French, early eighteenth century. All about one-third actual size. The plain ones were excavated in Northampton. (Northampton Museum.)

Small drug-pots, some decorated with simple painted patterns in blue, orange and purple, are early products which are common archaeological finds. In varying shapes they continued to be made throughout the seventeenth and eighteenth centuries (40-44). Besides these little pots, much other delft was made for apothecaries, including flat slabs either for rolling pills or for shop signs, and the larger drug jars, which are often dated, with inscriptions naming their contents (45 and 46).

These specialised wares were only a small part of the delft produced. Most delft was for use at the dining table or on the sideboard and consisted of plates, bottles, mugs, porringers and such like. Some vessels like the chargers may have been purely decorative (47-49). Although wares decorated with colour, either blue or polychrome, were produced from the start, a large proportion of delft was plain. These vessels, although most attractive with their plain thick white glaze, did not usually survive daily use and so are greatly under-represented in collections, but they are common archaeological finds. Bowls, chamber-pots, mugs, candlesticks, porringers (small handled bowls) and plates are common plain shapes, and many of these are also found with very simple decoration (38 and 39).

It is difficult to distinguish the delft made in London in the early seventeenth century from the Dutch wares, which were

Delft drug jars, both painted in two shades of blue. **45.** Dated 1680; the expanded inscription *S[yrupus] Sambucci baccae* means syrup of elderberries (height 162 mm). **46.** Dry drug jar; *Electuarium Lenitivium* means 'lenitive electuary', a laxative (height 185 mm). English, later eighteenth century. Both about one-third actual size. (Northampton Museum.)

themselves sometimes influenced by Italian majolica. From about 1630 distinctively English shapes were made, particularly bottles, mugs and posset pots. Some are decorated in imitation of Chinese porcelain, while others have more English styles. A little later the

Blue dash chargers. **47.** Tulip charger painted in yellows, browns, greens and, distressingly, blue tulips; lead-glazed on the back; Lambeth, about 1680 (diameter 331 mm). **48.** A rather grumpy-looking Queen Anne painted in two shades of blue with a little yellow and bright green, and sponged manganese trees; Bristol, about 1702-14 (diameter 300 mm). Both about one-sixth actual size. (Northampton Museum.)

49. Adam and Eve 'blue dash charger' painted mostly in blue, including the sponged trees, with a little greeny blue grass and fig leaves, and yellow fruit with orange features (diameter 352 mm). Very crazed, lead-glazed externally. Possibly Bristol, late seventeenth century. About a quarter actual size. **50.** Bowl painted in blue with a little dull dark green and tan (height 98 mm). London, about 1700-20. About half actual size. (Both Northampton Museum.)

so-called 'blue-dash' chargers began to be made, decorated with fruit, portraits — often royal (48), flowers — especially tulips (47), or Adam and Eve (49). These peculiarly English dishes continued to be made until the 1740s and are named after their blue-painted borders. The main decoration was painted in several colours. Until the 1690s the cheaper lead glaze was commonly used for the backs of these chargers.

During the eighteenth century the greatest influence on delft was Chinese porcelain, resulting in many slightly altered and adapted Chinese patterns (54). Dishes and plates continued to be the most common vessels made, but punch bowls were made rather than posset pots, and jugs and mugs changed shapes, often imitating silver vessels. Fashionable tea and coffee wares were produced. Names and other inscriptions are found (53), sometimes relating to current events such as elections. Bucolic inscriptions continued to appear, particularly on punch bowls, plates and puzzle jugs, for example, on a punch bowl dated 1728, *Drink faire / Dont Sware.*

Decoration painted in two shades of blue, sometimes after about 1680 with dark blue-green outlining, is very common and often copies Chinese patterns. From the middle of the eighteenth century English and chinoiserie landscapes and figures were painted in blue and are especially effective on plates (51). From

51. Bristol delft plate with a charming chinoiserie (Chinese-inspired) scene painted in two shades of blue (diameter 170 mm). A script *13* is painted in blue on the base; about 1760. One-third actual size. **52.** Intensely spotted pale coffee-brown ground with reserves painted in two shades of blue (diameter 222 mm). Lambeth, about 1750-75. About one quarter actual size. (Northampton Museum.)

53. Delft mug, painted in blue, including the inscription *MARY TURNER AGED 2 YEARS 14 DAYS SEP[TEMBE]R 2 1752*, and a red line on the rim (height 95 mm). Probably Bristol. About half actual size. (Fitzwilliam Museum, Cambridge.) 54. Delft plate painted with a common Chinese style in tan, green, yellow, manganese and dark blue (diameter 228 mm). Lambeth, mid eighteenth century. About one quarter actual size. (Northampton Museum.)

about 1740 another Chinese style, 'powder' ground colour, with areas reserved on, or protected from, the ground colour and then painted with a pattern, was used usually in blue or manganese, and rarely green or brown (52).

Delft tiles were made from the late sixteenth century onwards, but the bulk of the surviving tiles are eighteenth-century. They were painted, or decorated with prints by the specialist printing firm of Sadler and Green in Liverpool from the 1750s (see pages 47 and 48), but this technique was only very rarely used on delft vessels.

There is a great deal of dated delft but very little has inscriptions or any form of identification to indicate where it was made. However, there have been excavations at many of the factories and, together with the few pieces which do identify themselves by inscriptions, research has made it possible to attribute many pieces to their factory. The many dated vessels and the fact that much delft followed contemporary Chinese imports or silver shapes in style or decoration make dating a piece easier than attributing it.

Imports from the continent of Europe, of both high quality intricately decorated wares and simpler vessels, continued even after delft was made in Britain, especially during the seventeenth century but also into the eighteenth century. It is not surprising that the elaborate wares were imported, since the delft made in Britain was usually simpler than, and often imitated, the continental. It does seem odd that the plainer wares travelled so far, but transport by sea was easier than overland.

In the 1770s delft was eclipsed by a new white earthenware, creamware. Delft had always had several disadvantages: it chipped and crazed easily and was rather heavy. Creamware was light, strong and also cheaper. A few delft factories continued in small scale production into the nineteenth century, but then all production ceased.

55, 56, 57. Stoneware bellarmines, probably imported from Germany in the late seventeenth or early eighteenth century, with a variety of mottled tan surfaces (heights 194, 183 and 183 mm). All excavated in Northampton. About one-third actual size. (Northampton Museum.)

5
Stoneware

Brown stoneware

Stoneware is extremely hard pottery produced from clay which will fire to a very high temperature (1200-1250°C) and become impervious, unlike earthenwares, which need to be glazed to hold liquids. Salt-glazed stoneware is glazed by throwing salt on to the pots in the kiln during firing, forming a thin shiny coating with a pitted texture like orange peel. It is normally grey, but often the exterior is covered with an iron-rich wash which fires to a mottled tan.

Stoneware developed in Germany from high-fired earthenware in the late thirteenth century, and a small amount is found in Britain from the fourteenth century onwards. During the sixteenth century quantities of jugs and mugs were imported and bellarmine face jugs (55-57) (named after Cardinal Bellarmine, 1542-1621) and colourful cobalt (blue) and manganese (purple) decorated Westerwald mugs were very common from the mid seventeenth century into the eighteenth.

In the late seventeenth century John Dwight succeeded in producing stoneware in London and, although some bellarmines may have been produced there earlier in the century, this is the first successful stoneware factory in England about which we have any information.

Bottles and ale mugs were early Dwight products in brown stoneware; as well as huge presentation mugs (59) and storage jars (58), they continued to be made throughout the eighteenth century at several factories in London, although the shapes and decoration altered during this period. The sprigged (page 35) hunt running round the vessel and a punch-drinking scene were both very popular (both on 59). Similar stonewares were also made in Bristol from the early eighteenth century.

The Nottingham stoneware industry flourished throughout the eighteenth century. The products are easily distinguished from other stonewares (except the very similar Derbyshire wares) because they have a very smooth lustrous brown surface, generally not mottled, and the pots are often very thin. An enormous variety of forms was made, including jugs, bowls, mugs, teapots, tea caddies and even cups and saucers.

The earliest products include strange double-walled mugs, with the outer wall pierced (61). Loving cups with inscriptions

58. Stoneware pickle jar with sprigged decoration and incised inscription *George Bennison and Sarah Nov. 28 1752* (height 273 mm). About one quarter actual size. Made in London. (Fitzwilliam Museum, Cambridge.) **59.** Huge stoneware mug with sprigged decoration and impressed inscription *Thomas Triplett 1761* (height 256 mm). Made in London. About one-third actual size. (Northampton Museum.)

60. Nottingham stoneware marriage cup with rouletted bands around, comb-incised decoration, and the inscription *W. B Marhar Barber C. T. Cornelius Toft 1727/8 hand,* repeated partially on the opposite side (height 248 mm). About a quarter actual size. (Northampton Museum.)

commemorating marriages were made throughout the eighteenth century (60). Many vessels were decorated with incised patterns, often flowers, and lines of rouletting produced by running a patterned wheel over the surface; occasionally the whole pattern was rouletted. Charming mugs in the shape of bears were produced (see title page) with the fur suggested by 'bread crumbs' of clay. This technique was also used on simpler vessels.

Similar stonewares were made at several places in Derbyshire from around 1700, and there were also factories elsewhere in the north, and possibly in Scotland, during the eighteenth century. Staffordshire produced brown stoneware from around 1680, mainly mugs and cups. Often only the upper part of the vessel was covered with the brown wash, leaving the lower half grey.

Red stoneware

Red stoneware looks different from the brown stonewares already discussed, but it is similar in being fired to a high temperature and in being very hard. It looks like a fine red unglazed earthenware. Red stoneware was imported from China alongside porcelain in the later seventeenth century, and John Dwight succeeded in copying it, as well as other types of stoneware. The Elers brothers soon made this ware in London and then in Staffordshire, and it is difficult to distinguish between London and Staffordshire products, both made in the 1690s. Globular mugs rather like 61 but plain, mugs like 63, beakers and teapots were the principal forms made, and they were often ornamented with 'sprigged' prunus flowers or other designs (63). Sprigging is applied decoration which is made in small moulds

61. Double-walled 'carved' Nottingham stoneware mug, about 1690-1705 (height 102 mm). **62.** Small stoneware bottle, perhaps made in London in the early eighteenth century (height 103 mm). **63.** An unglazed red stoneware mug with sprigged figures and flowers made in London or Staffordshire about 1700 (height 105 mm). About one-third actual size. (Northampton Museum.)

and then attached to the vessel, or, as with these early vessels, small moulds pressed on to the pot (58 and 59). (See page 41 for eighteenth-century red stoneware.)

White stoneware

John Dwight succeeded in making white stoneware (along with many other varieties) in London in the late seventeenth century, using 'ball' clay from Dorset. This fine white clay was already being used to make clay pipes. However, Dwight only produced small quantities, and production on a commercial scale did not take place until the 1720s, and then in Staffordshire, not London. The first attempts at a white stoneware were made of the usual grey stoneware fabric dipped into the white clay. The earliest of these had the common brown wash over the top half of the vessels, often mugs, so that only the lower half was white. These were soon followed by vessels on which the white dominated (65). The dipped wares continued to be made until the 1760s because they were much cheaper, using local clay for the bulk of the pot and the expensive imported white clay only for the coating. Another economical stoneware, drab ware, made during

White stoneware. **64.** Chocolate pot enamelled in a Chinese style in several colours (height 146 mm). Staffordshire, about 1760s (the lid is a restoration). **65.** Stoneware mug with white dipped surface and a brown band on the rim (height 126 mm). Staffordshire, about 1720. Excavated in Northampton. Both a little under half actual size. (Northampton Museum.)

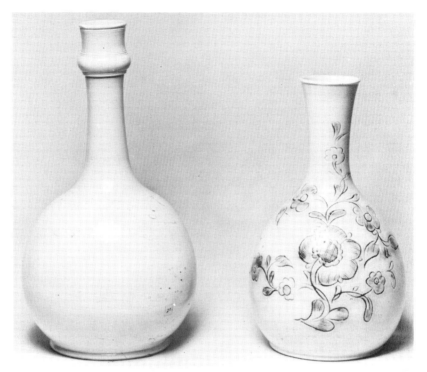

White stoneware bottles. **66.** Plain white, lathe-turned (height 266 mm). **67.** Scratch blue decorated (height 224 mm). Both Staffordshire, mid eighteenth century. About one-third actual size. (Northampton Museum.)

the 1720s and 1730s from a local Staffordshire clay which fired grey, was decorated with white clay sprigging. White stoneware, with the whole pot made from white clay, was developed around 1720. Calcined (burnt) ground flint was used in the fabric instead of sand and made the vessels very strong and light. White stoneware, like the brown, was glazed with salt.

This new lightweight pottery must be seen in relation to its contemporaries. The only comparable ceramics available were imported Chinese or continental porcelain, which was white but very expensive, and delft, either English or continental, which had an almost white appearance but was heavy and easily chipped. White stoneware was ideal for the growing middle-class market for newly fashionable tea wares, and for table pottery generally. Its sophistication is in marked contrast to the contemporary Staffordshire slipwares and stonewares, and its shapes

White salt-glaze. **68, 69.** Small starfish dishes made over a one-piece mould (both 71 mm across). **70.** Heart-shaped pickle tray, slip-cast (height 23 mm). **71.** A tiny pipkin, thrown and turned on the lathe (height 61 mm). All Staffordshire, mid eighteenth century. About one-third actual size. (Northampton Museum.)

relate more to contemporary silver than to the traditional shapes of slipware and earthenware. Large-scale production of white stoneware preceded porcelain manufacture in England by some twenty-five years.

Many of the early white stonewares were thrown on the wheel and then, when leather hard, turned on a lathe (66). Some were then decorated with sprigged ornaments. Much excavated white salt-glaze is plain and it includes fine tankards with simple ribbing, plain bowls and large jugs, as well as tea wares.

Press-moulding and slip-casting, two mass-production methods employed on white stoneware, were introduced during the 1740s. The results are similar, in effect producing the pot, or part of the pot, complete with its decoration in one operation, but the techniques are different.

For press-moulding, a thin sheet of clay was pressed into a single mould or was squeezed between the upper and lower parts of a two-part mould. White stoneware was so strong that very thin vessels could be produced in this way, and the thin salt-glaze did not blur the moulded details.

Slip-casting means that slip or liquid clay was poured into a plaster of Paris mould, which absorbed the water from the slip so that the vessel could be removed. With a complicated object such as a teapot the main body and the other parts — the spout, handle and foot-ring (if any) — would all be cast separately and then assembled. Exotic shapes were made by this method, including teapots in the form of houses, ships or camels. The quality of slip-cast vessels ultimately depended on the carved block from which the mould was made and on the condition of the working mould, whilst press-moulded vessels depended on the quality of the mould. With these methods, skilled work was required from the block cutter or mould maker, rather than from the potter himself.

White salt-glaze was also decorated in colour. Scratched decoration was infilled with blue stained clay (67) and occasionally with brown, and sometimes blue or brown sprigs were used. Occasionally vessels were completely covered with dark blue.

From about 1750 salt-glaze was enamelled (painted with colours) in imitation of contemporary Chinese or English porcelain. The fired vessel had to be refired at a lower temperature to fix the enamels. Gilding was also used from a slightly earlier date and was fixed at a still lower temperature. White salt-glaze took enamels very well, the crisp bright colours contrasting with the clean white body, and much of the painting was of a very high standard (64). While much enamelled ware was produced in Staffordshire, it is likely that plain Staffordshire vessels were also sent to be decorated elsewhere.

Staffordshire was the largest producer of white salt-glaze, but it was made in many other areas — Derbyshire, Yorkshire and Liverpool, for example — but attribution to a particular factory is difficult.

By around 1770 white salt-glazed stoneware was losing its popularity in the face of competition from the newly refined cream-coloured earthenware developed in Staffordshire, known as creamware.

White salt-glaze teapots. **72.** Painted with several coloured enamels, and with a crabstock handle and spout; Staffordshire, 1760s (height 128 mm). **73.** Heart-shaped slip-cast teapot with vine decoration and a snake head on the spout; Staffordshire, 1740s or 1750s (height 132 mm). Both about a quarter actual size. (Northampton Museum.)

Post-Medieval Pottery

Red-bodied jugs. **74.** Plain, unglazed, lathe-turned red stoneware with silver mounts (height 144 mm). **75.** Similar, but with sprigged motifs (height 144 mm). **76.** Glazed red earthenware with white sprigged motifs (height 122 mm). All Staffordshire, about 1740s or 1750s. About one-third actual size. (Northampton Museum.)

Coffee-pots. **77.** Unglazed, engine-turned red stoneware, with a mock Chinese seal mark under the base; Staffordshire or Yorkshire, 1770s (height 248 mm). **78.** Jackfield ware, with sprigging and gilding; Staffordshire, 1750s (height 243 mm): very similar white salt-glaze and tortoiseshell ware coffee-pots exist. Both about one quarter actual size. (Northampton Museum.)

6
Fine earthenwares

By the middle of the eighteenth century Staffordshire was producing a great variety of fine, lightweight and elegant lead-glazed earthenwares. A selection of fabrics — glistening black, red, orange, marbled and almost white — and numerous methods of decoration — white or coloured sprigs, coloured glazes, slip, rouletting and moulding — are found. Some of the motifs, like the vine or prunus, were simple, but many more formal sprigged motifs are found, and some very odd moulded designs. Many of the shapes and some of the decoration are similar to those on contemporary white salt-glaze; indeed occasionally they are identical.

There appears to be a gap in the production of unglazed red stoneware between about 1700 and about 1740. During the middle to late eighteenth century teapots, coffee-pots, jugs and mugs were made, some simply turned on the lathe for a beautiful smooth finish (74), others decorated with sprigged patterns (76) and some with rather strange overall incised zig-zag lines (77) produced by engine turning, that is mounting the vessel in a lathe and using a comb to incise the decoration. This method was also used on glazed red stoneware. Glazed red earthenware either with a white slip line on the rim or with simple white sprigged motifs (76) has been called 'Astbury' ware, after one of the potters known to have made this type of pottery.

Agate ware, made from differently coloured clays intermixed, is probably most effective in the simpler shapes like the cup and saucer (83), although complex teapots and other vessels were made. It was occasionally used for salt-glazed stoneware.

Less vibrantly coloured earthenwares were also produced; a pleasant orange with white sprigged flat flowers touched with colours is common, although other colours and styles were made.

One of the most startling fine earthenwares is the 'shining black' or 'Jackfield ware'. Although this is named after a place in Shropshire where some of it was made, the bulk of the ware was almost certainly produced in Staffordshire. Plain but beautifully made shapes like the mug (79) are very elegant and striking. It was also made with white or black sprigging, which is very effective (78, 81 and 82). Cold, or unfired, gilding and painting were also used, but much of this has now worn away. Enamelled decoration was also produced.

Mugs. **79.** Jackfield ware (height 163 mm). **80.** Agate ware (height 132 mm). Both thrown and turned on the lathe. Staffordshire, mid eighteenth century. Both about one-third actual size. (Northampton Museum.)

Fine earthenwares were also made outside Staffordshire, for example in Yorkshire and Shropshire, but it is difficult to distinguish these from the Staffordshire products.

Jackfield tea bowls and saucers. **81.** With black sprigged decoration. **82.** With white sprigs. Both gilded; Staffordshire (height 55 mm). **83.** Agate ware cup and saucer; probably Staffordshire (height 81 mm). All mid eighteenth century. About one-third actual size.'· (Northampton Museum.)

Josiah Wedgwood

There were many skilled potters working in Staffordshire but so far few of them have been referred to. This is partly because of lack of space, and partly because we know very little about many of them. However, Josiah Wedgwood has to be singled out. Staffordshire pottery was predominant before his time, but his scientific methods refined many of the wares, most notably creamware as described later. Of the fourth generation of Wedgwood potters, he was a partner of Thomas Whieldon from 1754 to 1759, making colour-glaze, agate, marbled and black wares. He then set up on his own, and when he died in 1795 he left the large firm which thrives today.

Basaltes

The hard black stoneware known as basaltes was produced from the middle of the eighteenth century and was sometimes called Egyptian Black. Wedgwood renamed it basaltes in the early 1770s, after refining it. Most basaltes was elaborately sprigged or engine-turned, or both, usually in classical styles. Some vessels were simply turned (85), and a small amount was painted with classical scenes or borders.

Its production was not limited to Wedgwood or even to Staffordshire. Vast quantities of basaltes tea and coffee wares were made in Leeds from around 1780, and many Staffordshire potters besides Wedgwood made it.

Jasper

The most famous ware made by Wedgwood is jasper, introduced in 1774 and still in production. This fine stoneware with white sprigged, usually classical, decoration was the result of four years' experiment by Wedgwood. He wanted to develop a ceramic which was capable of reproducing very fine detail, and he succeeded wonderfully. The earliest jasper was coloured right through the body, but this caused problems and later a surface dip was use. Many very sophisticated vases, medallions and even jewellery were made in blue, sage green, lilac, yellow or black jasper, but useful wares were also produced and were imitated by other potters. Much of the decoration is classical (84).

Wedgwood also developed red stoneware, renaming it 'Rosso Antico' about 1775. This was decorated with contrasting sprigged decoration or painted with formal classical borders. Another unglazed ware made from the 1780s, caneware, was pale brown, often elaborately moulded and sometimes painted as well.

Post-Medieval Pottery

84. Jasper teapot (height 130 mm), white body with a sage green dip and white sprigs, from a series called 'Domestic Employment'; this one is 'Sewing'. Stripes have been turned through to the white body towards the base. Impressed *WEDGWOOD* on the base. Staffordshire, 1780s. About one-third actual size. (Temple Newsam House, Leeds.)

85. Very plain classical basaltes teapot (height 135 mm). Impressed *WEDG-WOOD*. Staffordshire, about 1790-1810. About a quarter actual size. (Northampton Museum.)

86. Colour-glazed coffee-pot, with sprigged motifs splashed with green, brown and yellow in the glaze (height 168 mm). Identical pots are known in salt-glaze. Staffordshire, 1740s. **87.** Colour-glaze or tortoiseshell ware covered jug with a streaky brown glaze outside (height 176 mm). Staffordshire, 1740s or 1750s. Both about one-third actual size. (Northampton Museum.)

Whieldon or colour-glaze ware

An almost white earthenware, made with the same ingredients as white stoneware, was made in Staffordshire alongside the coloured-bodied earthenwares and white stoneware. It was fired to a lower temperature than stoneware and was glazed with lead, not salt. It is not certain when this ware was first made but it was in production in the 1740s.

Colour-glaze ware, and its direct descendant the whiter creamware, can be considered the ultimate development of the lead-glazed tradition of English potting. However, white stoneware was the first to use the ingredients of white ball clay and ground flints, and it is possible to see colour-glaze and creamware as simply the lead-glazed equivalent of the stoneware, since they were made from the same recipe. All these white wares were the British pottery industry's response to imported white porcelain. Thus the origins of creamware are complex.

Much of this ware was decorated with almost translucent colours actually in the glaze, produced by dusting on metallic oxides. These ran during firing (86), producing a rather blurred, messy effect unless they were used quite densely, as in 88, to produce what has been known as tortoiseshell ware. A beautiful green glaze, refined around 1760, was used to splendid effect on vessels modelled as cauliflowers, pineapples and other fruits (89 and 93).

88. Hexagonal teapot, slip-cast with a Chinese pattern, mostly green, with yellow, brown and grey (height 116 mm). Staffordshire, 1760s, perhaps Wedgwood. **89.** A cauliflower tea caddy, with green-glazed leaves (height 114 mm). Slip-cast, Staffordshire, 1760s. Both about one-third actual size. (Northampton Museum.)

Colour-glazed plates, all imitating silver forms and decoration. **90.** Grey-blue glaze with splashes of black, green and yellow. **91.** Octagonal, brown glaze with large spots of green and yellow. **92.** Black with much green and yellow. 90 and 92 are possibly Yorkshire, 91 Staffordshire, all about 1760s or 1770s (diameter of all three about 240 mm). About one-sixth actual size. (Northampton Museum.)

As with white salt-glaze, some shapes imitated metal prototypes — the three lion's masks and claw feet on 87 for example. Crabstock handles and spouts, imitating branches of trees, were common in all fine earthenwares as well as white salt-glaze (72). Colour-glazed wares avoided the extremes of salt-glaze: the cauliflower and chinoiserie (Chinese-inspired) slip-cast designs, although exotic, are very pretty.

Colour-glaze has been called Whieldon ware because Thomas Whieldon was known to have made it, along with almost every other type of fine earthenware and white stoneware. However, he was only one of the many potters making colour-glaze wares. As with all the fine earthenwares, production was not restricted to Staffordshire. In common with all the fine earthenwares of the mid eighteenth century, table wares, especially those for serving tea, coffee and chocolate, were common colour-glaze products. Plates and shallow dishes like 90 to 92 must have been produced in huge quantities, since great numbers survive and they are common excavated finds.

7
Creamware

The colour-glazed wares gradually evolved towards the fine white creamware, which became the most successful pottery ever made in England. It excelled porcelain in lightness and rivalled it in decoration, but it was much cheaper. Its success virtually put the delftware potters out of business even on the continent of Europe. Salt-glaze and other fine earthenwares had been exported from Britain, but creamware was sent to Europe and America in vast quantities.

Creamware made from Devon and Dorset ball clays, and decorated like the salt-glaze with enamel colours over the glaze, was being made in the 1750s alongside colour-glazed wares, in Staffordshire and elsewhere. Several Staffordshire potters were trying to improve it and make it paler. Wedgwood introduced Cornish china clay, which made the ware much whiter, and in 1765 Queen Charlotte ordered a creamware tea service from him: Wedgwood renamed his creamware 'Queen's Ware'.

Creamware was made in many other places besides Staffordshire. The Leeds Pottery was the largest. Colour-glazed and other fine earthenwares had been made there from around the middle of the eighteenth century, and from the 1780s quantities of very fine creamware were produced. Commonly Leeds handles on teapots and such like were double and intertwined, with small sprigged flowers concealing the junctions of the handle and body (94, 95 and 97), but similar types were also used in Staffordshire. There were also several smaller creamware factories in Yorkshire, two in Derbyshire (94), and others elsewhere, including Newcastle and Bristol. In Liverpool the Herculaneum Pottery made creamware, amongst other wares, and Sadler and Green printed designs on Wedgwood creamware from Staffordshire. Liverpool was very well placed for the large export trade to America.

Unlike salt-glaze, creamware had a smooth surface, very suitable for transfer printing. It seems strange to print on pottery, but by this method complex designs could be reproduced easily and cheaply. Intaglio copper plates were used: the plate was filled with colour, a mixture of metallic oxides, fluxes and oil: the impression was taken on to a piece of paper, applied to an already fired and glazed pot, and then fired on.

Much creamware, particularly plates, was decorated by this

93. Colour-glazed creamware coffee-pot, slip-cast as a cauliflower, partly green-glazed (height 244 mm). Staffordshire or Yorkshire, 1760s. 94. Creamware coffee-pot painted with coloured enamels, and with an elaborate handle and flower knob (height 245 mm). Melbourne, Derbyshire, about 1770. Both about a quarter actual size. (Northampton Museum.)

method from about 1760. From 1761 the firm of Sadler and Green in Liverpool, specialist ceramic printers, decorated Wedgwood creamware with prints, usually dark red, black or lilac. Most of the prints were left plain, but some were washed over with enamel colours. Printing was not introduced at the Leeds Pottery until around 1780.

Some of the early painted (enamelled) creamware is very similar to painted white salt-glaze, but much of it is in a distinctive and charming style (95 and 97). Other styles are similar to porcelain (99), and occasionally identical patterns were used (96 and 100). Very formal, modern-looking borders usually date from after 1770 (101).

Underglaze blue-painted decoration was used on creamware (96 and 99) in imitation of Chinese and English porcelain. Blue is so common because the pigment, cobalt, will stand the high temperatures needed to fire pottery or porcelain, and so can be applied to the unfired vessel. Other colours were more expensive to use because they were applied over the glaze and so needed an extra firing.

Plain, simple creamware was also produced (98), alongside all these decorated wares. Very splendid plain white creamware with moulded decoration was made in Staffordshire and Leeds,

Creamware teapots. **95.** Painted with coloured enamels in a typical creamware style (height 144 mm). Impressed *WEDGWOOD* on the base. Staffordshire, 1770s. **96.** Painted in underglaze blue with a pattern commonly found on Worcester porcelain (see 106) (height 163 mm). Possibly Leeds, 1780s. Both about a quarter actual size. (Northampton Museum.)

including large tureens, ewers, pierced dishes and plates, cruet stands complete with bottles and casters, and very elaborate centrepieces for dining tables with hanging baskets, or shells, around a central figure. Although plainer and more restrained, these creamwares are amongst the most sophisticated earthenwares of the eighteenth century. Jasper illustrates most clearly the later eighteenth-century interest in classical decoration, but many of the wares, including creamware, were influenced by the 'antique' Greek and Roman style.

Mugs. **97.** Creamware painted with large roses in coloured enamels with an elaborate handle and terminals (height 94 mm). Leeds or Staffordshire, later eighteenth century. **98.** Plain creamware (height 123 mm). Probably Staffordshire, 1790s. **99.** Pearlware painted in underglaze blue with a very common pattern (height 112 mm). Staffordshire or Leeds, later eighteenth century. All about a quarter actual size. (Northampton Museum.)

Pearlware. **100.** Small jug in an earthenware shape, but copying a New Hall porcelain pattern — see 112 (height 72 mm). Staffordshire, about 1790s. **101.** Coffee can (small cylindrical mug) impressed *WEDGWOOD* and painted pale and dark green (height 64 mm). **102.** Creamware mug printed on the glaze in black (height 91 mm). Liverpool or Staffordshire, about 1790s. All about one-third actual size. (Northampton Museum.)

From around 1770 potters, including Wedgwood, started to mark their wares. Earlier pots such as the Toft slipwares occasionally had names in the decoration, and little tally marks or potters' batch marks are found on many types of pottery, but for the first time clearly legible potter's or factory names were impressed on the underside of vessels. The amount of pottery marked varied from factory to factory: at Leeds it was only a very

Pearlware jugs. **103.** Slip-cast with *MISCHIEVOUS SPORT* this side and *SPORTIVE INNOCENCE* on the other (height 152 mm). Pratt ware, Staffordshire, about 1790s. **104.** Brown slip bands and blue lines top and bottom, with back chequering between (height 164 mm). Probably Yorkshire, about 1790. Both about one-third actual size. (Northampton Museum.)

small proportion, whereas it was more common at the Stafford-shire factories.

Printed pattern books illustrating the shapes available were issued by several potteries, including Leeds and Wedgwood, from the 1770s and 1780s, and along with the surviving manuscript pattern and shape books used in the factories they help with attributing the wares.

From 1779 a slightly blue-glazed variant of creamware — pearlware — was produced and was very popular into the nineteenth century. It was commonly decorated with underglaze blue prints or painted in imitation of porcelain (99 and 100). Pratt ware is a distinctive type of pearlware, decorated with high temperature colours. It was made in the late eighteenth century by Felix Pratt in Staffordshire but was copied by other potters in Staffordshire and elsewhere (103). From the late eighteenth century there was also a revival of slip decoration — either marbled or in bands (104).

Creamware and pearlware are the direct ancestors of modern white earthenwares.

105. Worcester porcelain mug printed in underglaze blue with a Chinese design, about 1760s (height 86 mm). **106.** Lowestoft porcelain tea caddy painted in underglaze blue, copying a Worcester pattern, 1780s (height 102 mm). The regularity of the print contrasts with the freely painted decoration. Both about half actual size. (Northampton Museum.)

English porcelain cups. **107.** Underglaze blue-painted, Lowestoft, about 1775-80 (height 60 mm). **108.** Moulded prunus blossom, Bow, about 1755 (height 60 mm). **109.** Printed over the glaze in black, Worcester, about 1770 (height 54 mm). **110.** Painted in underglaze blue, onglaze enamels and gilding, Worcester, about 1765-70 (height 60 mm). All about one-third actual size. (Northampton Museum.)

8
Porcelain

Even a brief survey of post-medieval pottery cannot ignore porcelain, although strictly pottery and porcelain are different materials. Porcelain is fired to a very high temperature and is white, very hard and usually translucent when held up to a light. It had a great influence on the development of pottery. White earthenwares like creamware or delft were trying to imitate this expensive ware, and porcelain shapes were copied not only in these white wares, but also in the coloured-bodied earthenwares. Only the local earthenware and slipware potters were immune, since their thick-bodied wares could not possibly imitate porcelain.

Porcelain was made in China from the ninth century AD, and when trading with the West began in the later sixteenth century blue-painted porcelain was exported to Europe. During the seventeenth century the trade increased, and enamelled porcelain and red stoneware were also sent. From the 1720s many purely European shapes and styles of decoration were made especially for export, including tea or dinner services with coats of arms.

European potters tried to imitate Chinese and Japanese porcelain, and the first successful large-scale factory was founded at Meissen in Germany in 1710. This produced the Chinese hard-paste porcelain made from kaolin (china clay) and felspar. During the early eighteenth century, other factories were set up all over Europe, some of which made the true hard-paste, while others made soft-paste. This was only made in Europe and is a successful imitation of Chinese porcelain using different ingredients. It looks warmer and softer than the hard-paste and was fired at a lower temperature. A great variety of recipes was used.

Porcelain production in England began about 1745 at Chelsea. There had been experiments in several places before this. Another London factory, Bow, and Bristol were established before 1750, and during the 1750s Derby, Worcester, Lowestoft and several small factories in Liverpool started manufacturing. Plymouth and Caughley (Shropshire) followed. Most of these made soft-paste porcelain of various types but true hard-paste was made at Plymouth and later at Bristol.

There was no royal or aristocratic patronage in Britain as there had been on the continent of Europe, and the factories were comparatively small. However, a great variety of shapes and

111. Globular Worcester porcelain teapot painted in underglaze blue bands with onglaze colours and gilding in the Queen's or Catherine Wheel pattern, about 1760s (height 131 mm). **112.** 'Silver shape' New Hall porcelain teapot painted with onglaze enamels in the 'cottagey' style, about 1785-95 (height 156 mm). Both about one-third actual size. (Northampton Museum.)

decorations was produced, even by a single factory, so that only a brief summary can be given here.

Many of the earliest wares were painted in underglaze blue in imitation of Chinese porcelain. Overglaze transfer printing, first used for enamels, occurs on porcelain from the late 1750s, in black and purple (109). Underglaze blue printing was developed in the 1760s (105). The only plain porcelain made was figures and vessels decorated with moulded patterns (108). From the earliest period onglaze painted enamels were used, both for imitations of Chinese decoration, and for European-style patterns, especially flowers (112). Some of the most effective patterns used are a combination of underglaze blue, onglaze enamels and onglaze gilding (110 and 111).

Some porcelain factories used marks, and since all of them used different styles of decoration and often different fabrics it is usually possible to attribute a piece of porcelain to its factory.

Although some early experiments were made there and in spite of the presence of the Longton Hall (1750-60) and New Hall (1781-1835) porcelain factories, Staffordshire was not a very important area for porcelain production until the nineteenth century. After Josiah Spode perfected bone china there around

1796 many Staffordshire firms started producing it. Bone china is porcelain made of hard-paste ingredients with 25 per cent or more calcined bone: this is the porcelain still in production today.

9
An early eighteenth-century pit group

This group shows the great variety of pottery found in one pit in Dorchester. The pots are illustrated by conventional archaeological finds drawings, which give much more detail than a photograph. On the left-hand side of each drawing is a section through the body of the pot, with any interior decoration. The right-hand side shows the outside of the pot. Where the pots are not round-bodied a plan is also drawn (for example, 13 and 14). The drawings make the pots look complete, but this is not so since only a full profile of the pot needs to survive in order for it to be drawn, and if the decoration is repetitive it can be fully reconstructed. Black is used in the drawings to indicate either white slip or blue-painted decoration. They are one-quarter life size.

This group is one of several found during an excavation at the Plume of Feathers, Dorchester, Dorset. 1-11 and 13 and 14 are all local earthenware. Their fabric is fine, slightly sandy and hard, with very occasional larger inclusions, and flecks of dark brown. These cause tiny streaks of dark brown in the glaze, which varies from a rather dull green overall on the mug (1), through olive green (6, 7, 9 and 11) or olive green with orange patches (3 and 8) to orangey brown with occasionally green patches (2, 4, 5, 10, 13 and 14). This variation is due to firing, and all the pots probably came from the same kiln. 2 to 11 have white slip which has glazed rather yellowy, and on 7 and 9 there are brown flecks in the glaze over the slip, suggesting that either the slip or the glaze was contaminated with flecks of iron.

All the slip decoration is sgraffito, done while the slip was wet. In some cases there are scratch marks where there is no slip or the slip is not glazed (11). The decoration has obviously been done quickly, but it is very effective.

12 and another identical pot not illustrated have a dark brown iron glaze. 21 is a small part of a moulded slipware dish, either from Staffordshire or Bristol, with white slip overall and one tan dot. The delft from this group includes a blue-painted plate (15) which is a unique variant of a well known delft pattern of the 1630s, the bird on the rock, derived from Chinese porcelain. This plate probably dates from the later seventeenth century. The plain delft punch bowl (16) is early eighteenth-century and was

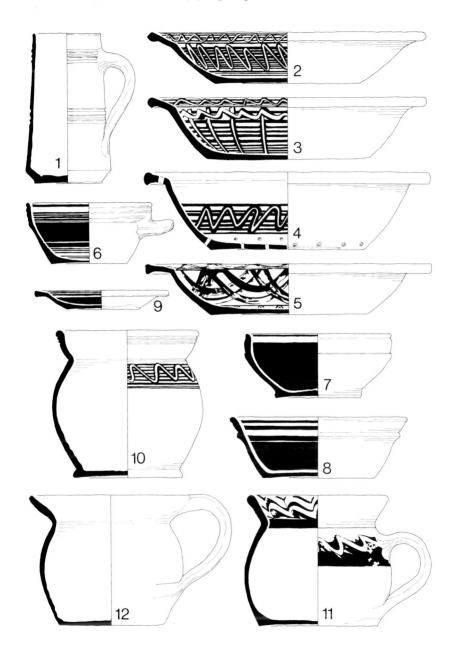

made in London or Bristol, while the octagonal tea bowl, painted with two shades of blue, came from Germany, perhaps Frankfurt. The stoneware bellarmines (18 and another not illustrated) and plain bottle (19) were also imports from Germany, as were the Westerwald tankards (20 and another not illustrated). 20 was made especially for the English market with AR for Anne Regina (1702-14).

Taking the clay pipes and glass bottles into consideration, we can say that this group was deposited around 1710-20, and that the delft plate (15) was old when it was broken and discarded. It is not uncommon to find 'heirloom' material in pit groups, and it is often either finer pottery or glass bottles.

It is clear that a local pottery kiln was supplying most of the pottery used and that the commonest forms were decorated dishes and bowls (another three are not illustrated) with or without handles. There are two other chamber-pots not illustrated similar to 17, but it seems that another pottery was supplying iron-glazed versions (12) since these differ in both shape and fabric from the others. The bulk of the non-local wares was imported from Germany, although there is delft from Bristol or London and slipware from Bristol or Staffordshire. Although Chinese porcelain was being commonly imported at this date there is none here; perhaps it was too expensive, or perhaps it was rarely used and well looked after.

The huge meat or dripping tray (13) weighed about 4 kilograms (9 pounds) and it is surprising that an identical one was excavated in Plymouth, where one would expect local Plymouth kilns to be supplying heavy pots like these. The similar smaller vessel (14) is a roaster, for cooking food in front of an open fire.

This group gives a good sample of the pottery in use in Dorchester in the early eighteenth century; elsewhere, even at the same date, there would be great differences in the pottery used, although the shapes might be broadly similar. For a complete picture of post-medieval earthenwares, pit groups from all over Britain and of all dates would be needed, together with study of the kilns and their products.

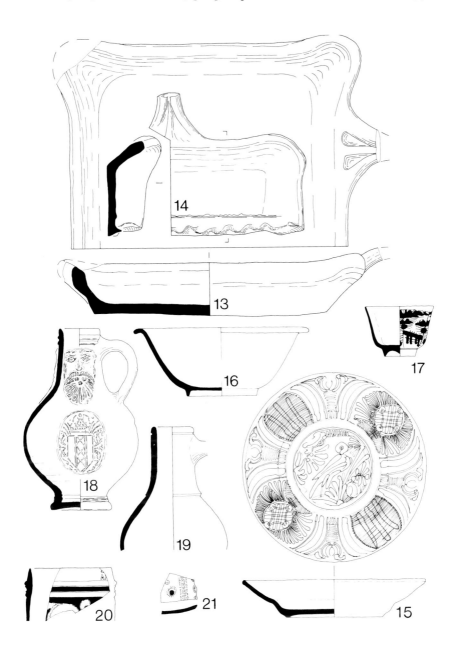

Further reading

Only a small selection of the many books and articles on ceramics can be given here, but many of those listed contain extensive bibliographies.

General
Charleston, Robert J. *World Ceramics: An Illustrated History.* Hamlyn, 1968.
Charleston, Robert J., and Towner, Donald. *English Ceramics 1580–1830.* Sotheby Parke Bernet, 1977.
Godden, Geoffrey A. *British Pottery: An Illustrated Guide.* Barrie & Jenkins, 1974.
Lawrence, Heather. *Yorkshire Pots and Potteries.* David & Charles, 1974.
Manners, Errol. *Ceramics Source Book.* Quantum Books, 1997.
Rackham, Bernard. *Catalogue of the Glaisher Collection.* 1934.
Rackham, Bernard, and Read, Herbert. *English Pottery.* 1924; reprint EP Publishing Ltd, 1972.
Rado, Paul. *An Introduction to the Technology of Pottery.* Pergamon Press, 1969.
Rhodes, Daniel. *Kilns: Design, Construction and Operation.* Cilton, 1968.
Weatherill, Lorna. *The Pottery Trade and North Staffordshire 1660–1760.* Manchester University Press, 1971.

Local earthenwares
Brears, Peter C.D. *The Collector's Book of English Country Pottery.* David & Charles, 1974.
Brears, Peter C.D. *The English Country Pottery.* David & Charles, 1971.
Lewis, J.M. *The Ewenny Potteries.* National Museum of Wales, 1982.
McGarva, Andrew. *Country Pottery – Traditional Earthenware of Britain.* A. & C. Black, 2000.
Archaeological journals, especially *Post-Medieval Archaeology* and the county journals.

Slipware
Cooper, R.G. *English Slipware Dishes*, Tiranti, 1968.
Grant, Alison. *North Devon Pottery.* Exeter University, 1983.
Wondrausch, Mary. *Slipware.* A. & C. Black, 1986.

Delft/tinglaze
Archer, Michael. *Delftware: The Tin-glazed Earthenware of the British Isles.* The Stationery Office, 1997.
Black, John. *British Tin-Glazed Earthenware.* Shire, 2001.
Garner, F.H., and Archer, Michael. *English Delftware.* Faber & Faber, 1972.

Further reading   61

Ray, Anthony. *English Delftware Pottery ... in the Ashmolean Museum, Oxford.* Faber & Faber, 1968.

Stoneware
Hildyard, Robin. *Browne Mugs: English Brown Stoneware.* Victoria and Albert Museum, 1985.
Lockett, T.A., and Halfpenny, P.A. (editors). *Stonewares and Stone Chinas of Northern England to 1851.* Stoke-on-Trent Museum, 1982.
Mountford, Arnold R. *The Illustrated Guide to Staffordshire Salt-Glazed Stoneware.* Barrie & Jenkins, 1971.
Oswald, Adrian, Hildyard, R.J.C., and Hughes, R.G. *English Brown Stoneware.* Faber & Faber, 1982.

Creamware
The Castleford Pottery Pattern Book 1796. EP Publishing Ltd, reprinted 1973.
Towner, Donald. *Creamware.* Faber & Faber, 1978.
Walton, Peter. *Creamware and Other English Pottery at Temple Newsam House, Leeds.* Manningham Press, 1976.
Northern Ceramic Society. *Creamware and Pearlware.* Stoke-on-Trent, 1986.

Porcelain
Godden, Geoffrey A. *English China.* Barrie & Jenkins, 1985.
Halfpenny, Pat, and Lockett, Terry (editors). *Staffordshire Porcelain 1740–1851.* Stoke-on-Trent Museum, 1982.
Sandon, Henry. *The Illustrated Guide to Worcester Porcelain.* Herbert Jenkins, 1969.
Vainker, S.J. *Chinese Pottery and Porcelain from Prehistory to the Present.* British Museum Press, 1991.

The pottery inscriptions quoted all come from *Early English Pottery: Named, Dated and Inscribed* (1891; EP Publishing Ltd, reprint 1973) by J.E. and E. Hodgkin. The inventories are taken from *Probate Inventories and Manorial Excerpts of Chetnole, Leigh and Yetminster* by R. Machin (Bristol University, 1976). For marks, see *Encyclopedia of British Pottery and Porcelain Marks* by Geoffrey A. Godden (Barrie & Jenkins, second edition 1991).

Places to visit

The museums listed here have very good displays of post-medieval ceramics, but most county and local museums have some local earthenware on display. Intending visitors are advised to check the times of opening before travelling.

Ashmolean Museum of Art and Archaeology, Beaumont Street, Oxford OX1 2PH. Telephone: 01865 278000. Website: www.ashmol.ox.ac.uk

Castle Museum, Norwich, Norfolk NR1 3JU. Telephone: 01603 493625. Website: www.norfolk.gov.uk/tourism/museums

Central Museum and Art Gallery, Guildhall Road, Northampton NN1 1DP. Telephone: 01604 238548.

Fitzwilliam Museum, Trumpington Street, Cambridge CB2 1RB. Telephone: 01223 332900. Website: www.fitzmuseum.cam.ac.uk

Manchester City Art Galleries, Mosley Street, Manchester M2 3JL. Telephone: 0161 234 1456. Website: www.cityartgalleries.org.uk

The Potteries Museum and Art Gallery, Bethesda Street, Hanley, Stoke-on-Trent, Staffordshire ST1 3DW. Telephone: 01782 232323.

Royal Albert Memorial Museum, Queen Street, Exeter, Devon EX4 3RX. Telephone: 01392 665858. Website: www.exeter.gov.uk/leisure

Temple Newsam House, Temple Newsam Road, off Selby Road, Leeds LS15 0AE. Telephone: 0113 264 7321. Website: www.leeds.gov.uk (Closed for redevelopment until Easter 2003.)

Victoria and Albert Museum, Cromwell Road, South Kensington, London SW7 2RL. Telephone: 020 7942 2000. Website: www.vam.ac.uk

Index